a sweet toned lullaby

a sweet toned lullaby
selected poems

by Wava Lee Caddenhead Fick

edited by Dale Marie Fick Campbell

Dallas: Tuckapaw Media
2010

a sweet toned lullaby: selected poems
by Wava Lee Caddenhead Fick
edited by Dale Marie Fick Campbell

Dallas, Texas: Tuckapaw Media, 2010
http://tuckapaw.com

ISBN-13: 978-0982069837
ISBN: 0982069839

Contents

Introduction

by Dale Marie Fick Campbell

My mother has been a poet since her high-school years. She was born Wava Lee Caddenhead in Dekalb, Bowie County, Texas, on November 16, 1929. Her parents separated soon after her birth, and her mother, Zula Marie Qualls Caddenhead, raised her in New Boston as a single mother in the midst of the Great Depression.

Some of the earliest poems in this collection were written during her high-school years in New Boston. The first of her high-school poems in this collection begins with the line, "The rain is falling o'er the town / Like a sweet toned lullaby..." I have taken the phrase "a sweet toned lullaby" as the title for this collection.

My mother attended the First Methodist Church of New Boston, and it was through her church connections that she learned about Lon Morris College, where she matriculated in 1947. Lon Morris instructors nurtured her poetic gifts and encouraged her to submit one of her poems to a national peer-reviewed journal of poetry by college students, *America Sings*. As a result, one of her poems was published in *America Sings* for the year 1951.

Lon Morris friends became her best friends. Through the years they gathered together, traveled together, celebrated and grieved together. They remain her closest and dearest companions. A particular group of Lon Morris friends called themselves "The Unholy Four" (Wava, Relta Buffington Turner, Mary Lou Goins Danheim, and Bonnie McCurdy High) and one section of poems in this book is dedicated to this group and their families.

It was also at Lon Morris College that my mother met her future husband, Carl Leroy Fick. They overlapped at the College for a year before Wava left for the University of Texas in 1949. My father soon followed her to UT and they were married at University Methodist Church on the UT campus on July 5, 1952. I showed up a year and a half later, in February 1954, the first of their seven children.

Children became the main focus of her life as Mama cared for her five daughters and two sons. She became a talented chef, seamstress and gracious hostess to the many, many friends and family who were constantly welcomed into her home. Grandchildren have become a new source of love for my mother. As her poetry shows, she is able to see the personalities of her grandchildren and express them perfectly in the poems she has written for each of them. Friends at Westbury United Methodist Church and at the United Methodist Center where she worked also became recipients of her poetic talent. On many different occasions she once again used her skills to celebrate people she knew.

This book is only a small sample of the many poems Wava Lee Caddenhead Fick has written over her life. I hope you will enjoy this selection and help celebrate her talent.

I want to especially thank my husband, Ted Allen Campbell for his invaluable help in making this book possible. I also want to thank Leah and Costas Tzimourakas for their help in making this book of poetry available.

December 2010

Family

To Edith, on Becoming Twenty-One
-Reflections

Another year has been consumed
By sharp, demanding teeth of Time,
Leaving only at its finish
Fragments of the meal sublime.
Carefully shall I take the pieces,
Place them in my heart to stay,
Precious bits that Time has left me
For a souvenir display.
Memories of the countless hours,
Spent in work and recreation,
A vision of the little chapel
Full of strength and inspiration.
In memory once again I wander
On a rolling, sun-kissed beach,
I stroll along a cobbled pathway-
Finding love within my reach.
Though the days so quickly vanished
They left me gasping at their haste,
From each hour I have gathered
Seeds that shall not go to waste.
I have kept the seeds of kindness,
Planted by some friend who cared;
And in turn I now shall reap them-
Deeds of kindness to be shared.
I have too the seeds of patience
That grew slowly in the soil,

But the roots spread strong and sturdy,
Watered oft with sweat of toil.
One quiet moment, in contrition
I plucked Faith's pure fragrant flower,
And true love, the sweetest blossom
I possessed one moonlit hour.

This is true! Another year has gone;
Before my very eyes in it fled,
And left me dreaming, ere it vanished
Of the lovely year ahead.

Our love to you,
Wava and Carl

For Dale

Though she is petite and dainty,
Within her heart there lies
A spirit that's strong and solid
And never can be compromised.

She gives herself to serve others,
To ease their burdens and pain;
And oft her kind words bring a healing
Like the cleansing of a soft rain.

She's a dear loving wife and good mother,
A friend that is tried and found true;
She challenges all of her students
To be the best in all they pursue.

The years have been kind in their passing,
For she has aged with much grace;
And there's strength and faith and beauty
Reflected in her smiling face.

May God continue to bless her
And be by her side every day;
May He look upon her with favor
As she strives to walk in His way.

February 6, 2002

For Elizabeth

You always have a happy smile
That glows like a nice surprise
What thoughts are flashing in your mind
And reflecting in your eyes.

Your life is full of many things-
Of school and Scouts and fun.
Of hobbies and special friendships
And projects to be done.

The days are passing much too fast,
These teenage years are near,
An with them comes confusion
And a tiny touch of fear.

Next comes high school and college,
And then will come the time
To test your wings and follow your dreams
And find a mountain to climb.

Remember all that you've been taught
Of faith and hope and love,
Then you'll be blessed in every way
By your Heavenly Father above.

For Lydia

With a careless shake of wind tossed curls
And a gleam in sparkling eyes
Is she a golden angel
Or Miss Mischief in disguise.

To her, life's an adventure.
Each day brings something new;
No matter it it's cold and dark
Or the sky is bright and blue.

Her tender heart is full or love
And the tears quite often flow.
She has a spirit firm and strong
And a mind to stretch and grow.

Oh golden girl, what is the secret
Nestled in your heart,
What yearnings do you seek to fill
As the walk of life you start.

May you wrap faith's cloak around you
As you journey on life's way;
May angels guide your every step.
May you feel God's love each day.

For Lydia
on Becoming Fifteen

You're at that very puzzling stage
Of being twixt and tween;
The time of womanhood is near,
Yet you are still a teen.

So many questions looming
And challenges to face;
Priorities that need sorting
Into their proper place.

There's character to be molded
And morals to be instilled;
A soul to find an anchor
And a dream to be fulfilled.

You are our country's future,
This generation's hope;
May you find strength and wisdom
And skills that help you cope.

As you celebrate your birthday
With lots of fun and laughter,
May God's great gift of love be felt
For now and ever after.

September 25, 2001

7

For Gloria

Like a breath of fresh air, refreshing and sweet
That touches the brow and scatters the heat,
She enters a room with a warm smile to share,
And eases a pain or lightens a care.
Committed to family, she works hard to build
A home where both love and dreams are fulfilled.
To work with the soil brings her great joy and
pleasure,
And always the yield brings a harvest of treasure.
She's a wonderful teacher with patience untold,
Digging for knowledge as a miner hunts gold.
Her husband and children all think she's the "best";
Her faith keeps her strong when she's put to the test.
Though birthdays do come as time marches on,
Each year grows more precious before it is gone;
Leaving behind sweet memories that last,
Etched in the record of all that is past.
May God grant her peace and goodness and love,
As He showers His blessings from heaven above.

January 10, 2002

For Greg

When he was young he thought as a child,
In pursuit of fun and play;
But now that he's become a man,
Those things are all put away.

Today, priorities are pressing
To claim his strength and his mind;
And he must choose what is lasting
And the things he will leave behind.

Though he knows not what lies ahead,
With hope he'll face each day;
Secure in faith, he's confident
That God will lead the way.

What treasures might be his to claim,
To enrich and bless his life;
A career that brings him much pleasure,
Or a loving, faithful wife.

God grant him both peace and patience,
Give him kindness, gentleness and love;
May his heart be o'erflowing with goodness,
All gifts from his Father above.

March 3, 2002

For Greg

More than a boy, he's not yet a man.
With confusing emotions he can't understand.
Growing quite tall and sturdy of limb,
A voice that is deep and a waist that is thin.
Those bright days of childhood are now put away.
Those innocent days of laughter and play.
Now thoughts of the future star; filling his brain,
 And unanswered questions just seem to remain.
The hours are passing more quickly, it seems
And looming ahead are new goals and dreams
Unafraid he will walk the straight path each day
For a strong inner spirit will show him the way.
Then swiftly the days will slip into years
With all of life' s pleasures and troubles and tears
And he'll oft remember that bittersweet time
When life seemed to have no reason or rhyme
And he was in limbo, twixt terror and joy
Not yet a man but more than a boy.

For Brian

He's the middle child in a trio of boys,
He's known hand-me-downs and slightly used toys,
With his little brother, he can't be too rough
Older brother's larger and stronger and tough.
Sometimes it 's hard to be number two,
A fellow can't always know just what to
He's a sensitive young man and a little bit shy
And sentimental stories ,just might make him cry.
But when it comes to reading, a champion he is
He's breaking all the records and he's really a whiz.
History or adventure or whatever he might find
Is eagerly absorbed into his fertile mind.
He is very athletic, he's an all around boy,
And he is his parents pride and joy.
There is a great advantage to being number two,
Because his older brother can show him what to do.
And he can be the model and help to point the way
For little brother's footsteps to safely walk each day.

For Brian

Walking toward the door of manhood,
Wondering now what he might find;
A few more years and he will enter,
Leaving childhood far behind.

So many challenges are waiting,
So many answers to be found;
What direction must he follow
As he walks on virgin ground.

He's prepared to take life's journey,
Sure of step and lack of fear;
In preparation for the future
He has stored the proper gear.

Running made him strong of body,
Faith is there to feed his soul;
Hope gives rise to focused vision,
Prayer will help him reach the goal.

May God bless him on this birthday,
Eighteen years to celebrate;
May the days ahead be golden,
And may joy and love await.

December 7, 2001

For Bruce

He's a bundle of energy with a gleam in his eye
And a great big mischievous grin.
He's always ready to join in a game
The question is not what, but when.
With two older brothers he tries to compete
And to prove that he really is tough
And he loves nothing better
    than for mom to complain
That the game is getting too rough
Life's an adventure, a free, happy time.
There is always plenty of fun.
A book to be read, a ball to be thrown
Or a challenging race to be run.
Those bright golden days full of laughter and joy
Make memories so precious and dear,
That even when time dims the eye and the mind,
The enchantment of childhood is near.

For Jeffrey on Turning Six

He helps his Mama garden,
And he likes to help her cook;
Goes fishing with his brothers
And loves to read a book.

He is his Daddy's shadow
And helps him if he can;
He's learning from example
On how to be a man.

A special day has now arrived
For a very special boy;
It's time for cake and ice cream
And lots of birthday joy.

Jeffrey now is turning six,
A brand new, happy year;
For him, life's just beginning
And the future holds no fear.

God ever bless and keep him
As he sleeps and as he wakes;
Help him grow in love and faith,
And guide each step he takes.

For Melissa on Her Birthday

It makes a mother's heart with pleasure beat
To claim a lovely daughter such as she;
Endowed with grace and beauty from within,
She stretches to embrace all she can see.

Her inner strength and beauty does reflect
The confidence that is her natural trait;
And she is ever challenged to complete
Each given task, if it be small or great.

A loving mother and a loyal wife,
She strives to fill the family's every need;
Yet reaches out to any who might call,
And answers with a kindly act or deed.

How did the years so very swiftly pass,
Transforming her within the frame of time
From curly headed babe with twinkling smile
To gracious lady living in her prime.

On this most special day of days,
When she is honored with the gift of love;
May God protect her with His tender care,
And shower her with blessings from above.

August 25, 2002

For Casey

You're a lovely little princess
With eyes of chocolate brown;
A smile that brightens up a room
And turns gloom upside down.

The world with all its beauty
Lies waiting at your feet,
And soon you will be ready
Its challenges to meet.

In a twinkle, little princess,
A lovely queen you'll be,
Then childish things will vanish
And new dreams you will see.

Oh take with you the wonder,
The innocence and joy
That only comes with childhood
And nothing can destroy.

For when the clouds are stormy
And life is full of fears,
In memory you can then return
To those happy, golden years.

For Kyle

With total concentration
You sit absorbed in play,
Oh tell me, towhead dreamer,
What is your trade today?

Are you a mighty engineer
Who guides a shiny train,
Or the pilot of a jumbo jet
That flies through clouds and rain.

Your cars are lined all in a row
Awaiting your command,
Then one by one they roll along,
Exactly as you planned.

With skillful hands you use your tools
To build or to repair.
Each detail is important
And needs your special care.

What will you be when you grow up,
My little towhead guy,
When childish games are over
And manhood hovers nigh.

May all those childhood memories
Be oft recalled with joy,
Those days when life was perfect
In the eyes of a little boy.

Wava Fick
August 1994

To Kyle
on Turning Twelve

It doesn't seem so very long
When you were just a tyke;
Learning how to take a step,
Then riding on a bike.

When did you grow so strong and tall,
Where have those years all gone;
Ere long you'll be a strapping teen
And then you'll be all grown.

Til then there's school with projects due
And sports and games to play;
Deadlines to beat and friends to meet
And chores to do each day.

But soon you will go looking
For what the future holds;
You'll choose the things of value
As you pick and choose your goals.

May God's eternal goodness
Be with you all your days;
May you be blessed with wisdom
As you e'er walk in His ways.

May 2, 2002

For a fleeting moment you were mine,
Sweet child of peace and rest;
Shrouded in hope, nestled in love,
A heart beat neath my breast.

So swiftly did you slip away
With the speed of quickened breath,
That only a shadow, lone and stray
Remains to fan the ache of death.

Lest I should weep, sweet babe of destiny
Because from earthly home you did depart,
Let me remember that throughout eternity
You chose to live instead within my heart.

Written between 1957-1959 after a miscarriage
between Melissa and Milton.

For Milton on His Birthday

Every Mother's prayer is for a son,
And you were sent to fill our lives with joy;
From babyhood, you very soon became
An energetic, lively little boy.

The years passed by with unrelenting speed,
All filled with happy times of work and play;
School and friends and church and chores to do,
Did fill each hour of your busy day.

Then all too soon you grew into a man,
And put behind the childish things of old;
Endowed with faith and trust and confidence,
You faced the future, unafraid and bold.

God blessed you with the bounty of His love,
And gave to you a faithful, Christian wife
To be a helpmate and a friend;
And walk beside you on the path of life.

Then God increased the bounty he bestowed
By giving seven children to your care;
To nourish them and teach them of His way,
Five handsome sons and two sweet girls so fair.

May this, your special day, be filled
With gentleness and goodness and with peace;
May all your troubles fade away,
And your happiness continue to increase.

August 27, 2002

For Diane

A wife of noble nature
With strength and honor dressed;
Her husband doth respect her
And her children call her blessed.

She does good work for others,
Provides for kith and kin;
She fears not for the future
But faces what life sends.

She has insight for choosing
Priorities of great worth;
She plants them in her children
Like seeds put in the earth.

Charm fools and beauty crumbles,
They fade like evening's light;
But her fear of God is wisdom,
And praiseworthy in His sight.

God bless her with His favor
And grant her love and peace;
May her cheeks be brushed with sunshine,
And her laughter never cease.

September 21, 2001

For Alex

Blessings to you, child of God
On this most special day;
May bounteous pleasures come to you
And troubles fade away.

Fair of face and quick of smile,
You charm whoe'er you meet;
Within your heart that beats so strong,
Lies no hate or deceit.

Fervent in nature and spirit,
You champion the things that are right;
Like a soldier going to battle,
You stay to fight the good fight.

Today you stand on the threshold
Of a future so golden and bright;
When you come to a fork in the highway,
May you choose the path that is right.

May your heart be full of contentment,
Your days be surrounded by love;
May treasures from heaven be granted
By your gracious Father above.

December 28, 2001

For Meredith
on Her Eleventh Birthday

Like a young gazelle so graceful,
O'er grassland bounding free;
Or a butterfly that's flitting
From bud to flowering tree;
She glides across the lighted stage
In costume shining bright;
And dances like a fairy,
All shimmering in the light.
When she dives into the water
With scarce a ripple stirred,
She is a sketch of youthful skill
By competition spurred.
Her heart is warm and full of love,
She seeks to do kind deeds;
She helps care for her siblings
Whenever they have needs.
She's growing in faith and beauty,
So lovely in every way;
May God be ever near her,
And guide her every day.

April 23, 2002

Garrison

Behind a quiet demeanor
Lies a spirit strong and free;
Just waiting for direction
To his future destiny.
Behind a smile so sweet and shy
A sense of humor hovers;
Bringing forth a bit of wit
A mischievous grin then covers.
Athletic skill he does possess,
He's lanky, fast and tall;
Baseball, football, basketball, track,
He's a champion in them all.
With a heart devout and faith that's strong,
The right path he is taking,
With a future rich with promise,
His success is in the making.

April, 2010

For Marcella
on Her Sixth Birthday

She's full of pep and vigor,
And her energy has no end;
She has a hard time choosing
Which project to begin.

When she has a dance recital,
She's a picture to behold;
As she bows and glides across the stage,
So graceful and so bold.

She loves to help her grandma cook,
To measure and to pour;
And to lick the bowl is yummy,
Too bad there isn't more!

Her life is just beginning,
With its mysteries to reveal,
As she walks into the future
With confidence and zeal.

May her life be full and happy,
And her faith be strong and sure;
May joy always surround her
And peace and love endure.

May 2, 2002

For Jared

He's such a happy little guy
With a great big smile and a gleam in his eye;
All it takes to bring him simple pleasure
Is a brand new car to add to his treasure.
Now it's time to honor this birthday boy
With cake and presents and lots of joy.
Secure and innocent, he looks ahead,
At four he has no fear or dread.
What dreams now nestle in his mind;
What future challenge might he find.
Will he become a race car driver,
Or choose to be a deep sea diver.
A preacher or doctor would be quite nice,
Or maybe a chemistry professor at Rice.
Will he be a lawyer like his Dad;
An engineer would make Grandpa glad.
Whatever his choice, may God guide his way;
Protect and keep him, each night and day.
May his life be filled with goodness and peace;
May God's richest blessings forever increase.

November 11, 2001

For Major

A wee young lad with laughing eyes
And a shy little smile has he;
Surrounded by love of kith and kin,
He's as blessed as one can be.

Innocent and free without a care,
To him it matters not
If the sky is dark and cloudy,
Or the sun is bright and hot.

Each day is a new adventure,
A door that is open wide
To a room with wondrous treasures
That are waiting just inside.

Ah, sweet is the life of a baby,
To be so happy and free;
To harbor no hate or resentment,
But live in sweet harmony.

God bless and help this little one,
And when he is mature,
May he keep the faith of a little child
Whose trust is strong and sure.

January 12, 2002

Rex

Life was made for a little boy
To run and jump and play;
To find some new adventure
And strength to test each day.
He's loving and snuggling and hugging,
And his smile is as bright as the sun;
He loves to play ball and that is not all,
For he's found that reading is fun.
Six siblings he has and he is the last,
So there's lots of affection to share;
And when there's some trouble,
They all come on the double;
There is always someone to care.
May the good Lord smile upon him
With rich blessings from above,
May every day that he may live
Be filled with joy and love.

April, 2010

For Leah

While still a tiny toddler,
A passion burned inside;
To find a new adventure
Or something yet untried.

Sometimes she burned her finger
And often stubbed her toe;
For her it taught a lesson
On things that she should know.

When she became much older,
There were choices to be made;
Which ones would be noble
And which ones would degrade.

She found her place in teaching,
Where young minds could be filled;
Where knowledge and direction
And ideals were instilled.

And now she is a mother
With three young lives to guide;
To help them find a future
Where faith and trust abide.

May she drink a cup of contentment
And dine at a table of love;
She is a pearl of great treasure
From God's vast storehouse above.

October 11, 2001

For Milton (T)

With twinkling eyes and sly little smile
He's eager to start each day;
No matter if it's sunny
Or if the sky is grey.

Sharp of mind and quick to find
A question he can ask,
He's rather read a story book
Than be assigned a task.

He likes to tease his sister,
His little brother too;
But he really has a loving heart,
And good deeds he will do.

A very happy birthday wish
For a young man now turned eight;
May all his candles sparkle
And his special day be great.

May God be ever present
To love and keep him near;
To give him faith and wisdom
And wipe away each tear.

For Evie

She's a dainty little pixie
With a flowing crown of hair;
Each new day's a gift to open,
Wrapped in love and free from care.

School is such a grand adventure,
Learning numbers, singing loud;
Bringing home a colored picture
That will make her Mama proud.

With two brothers she's not lonely,
And the three of them have fun;
But when she wants to play with Barbies,
She finds she's the only one!

Who will meet this lovely princess
As she walks the road of life;
Will she find a prince awaiting,
Just to claim her as his wife.

May God bless and ever keep her
On the straight and narrow way;
May His blessings, like a river
Flow around her every day.

November 5, 2001

For Michael

He never walks when he can run,
'Cause walking is too slow;
So many things for him to do,
And places he must go.

He loves to play with all his cars
And help by doing chores;
Go shopping with his Mama
And scope out all the stores.

Soccer is his favorite game,
He really loves to play;
And going to church on Sunday
Is the best part of the day.

A special day of honor
For him is very near;
A day of fun and presents,
And lots of birthday cheer.

May peace surround him always,
May he find joy and love;
May his steps be ever guided
By his heavenly Father above.

November 4, 2001

For Jana... Just Because

Like a beam of shimmering sunlight
Whenever she enters a room,
She brightens the corners of darkness
And chases away all the gloom.

Her smile, so warm and delightful
Brings hope wherever she goes;
Reflecting her sweet, gracious spirit
And the generous love she bestows.

She is a most thoughtful daughter,
A committed mother and wife;
Her faith sustains and directs her
To lead an exemplary life.

In the garden of life she is blooming,
A flower so fragrant and fair;
She brings joy to all those who touch her,
For it's God who has planted her there.

October 10, 2001

For Jana and Glenn
on Their Anniversary

Sixteen years ago they married
As they joined both hands and heart;
And they vowed to one another,
Not until death will we part.

They have faced each day together
Throughout all the passing years;
Sharing many happy moments,
Learning how to smile through tears.

Two dear children came to bless them
And to make their lives complete,
Though they brought new obligations
And fresh new challenges to meet.

There was character to be molded.
And high morals to instill;
A faith to make them pure in spirit
As their own dreams they fulfill.

May God bless you and your children,
May your goals in life be won,
May you tread life's path together
Until you face life's setting sun.

March 22, 2002
Wava Fick

For West

He's the twinkle in his mother's eye
And his Daddy's pride and joy;
His little sister's proud of him,
For he's a special boy.

He's very good in many sports,
But baseball he likes best,
As hitter or as catcher,
He's a head above the rest.

His Grandma loves to cook for him,
His Grandpa likes to tease;
And when he flashes those dark eyes,
He charms them to their knees.

And now a special day has come
When birthday candles shine;
A day to laugh and celebrate,
For West is turning nine!

May God be near to guide you,
In all you say and do;
May blessings fall like raindrops,
And all your dreams come true.

September 16, 2001

For West

With dimpled cheek and skin so fair,
You look with wondering eyes
To see what each new day will bring;
What unexpected prize.
So innocent do things appear
Through the eyes of a little boy,
No thought of hate or evil,
But only love and joy.
The days are hastening swiftly by
And flowing into years,
And soon will come awareness
Of sadness and of tears.
Oh fret not, precious little child
When the night grows dark and drear,
For a mother's love will hold you close
And a dad will calm the fear.
Above a star will shine its light
As a bright moon climbs a peak,
And the gossamer flutter of angel wings
Will softly brush your check.

For Roxanne

Sweet smiling babe with glowing eyes,
What brings such joy and mirth?
Is it some hidden secret
Revealed to you at birth?

As you kick your chubby little legs,
Does a vision fill your eyes
Of roads as yet untraveled?
Of a peak where an eagle flies?

Will life unfold to find you
In a mystic land so far?
Or will you be an astronaut
And speed to a distant star?

You may be a lovely princess,
Or a nurse or a farmer's wife;
So many gifts await you
In the treasure; chest of life.

For now, dear precious little babe,
I shall hold you very tight,
Before the years too quickly pass
And you walk into the night.

For Roxanne
on Her Eighth Birthday

What a wonderful day to honor
A birthday girl so sweet;
So bring on the cake and presents
And we'll all give her a treat.

To know her is to love her,
She's so gentle and so kind;
She has more friends than the law allows,
And good friends are hard to find!

Her days are filled with happy things;
Gymnastics, sports and school,
And playing with her big brother-
Now that is really cool!

She loves her kitten, Pixie,
And Katy, her Lab, is fun;
Her Mom and Dad adore her,
She is Daughter Number One!

May the Lord's face shine upon her
And guide each step she takes;
May angels ever watch her
As she sleeps and when she wakes.

March 23, 2002
Wava Fick

For Randall
on His Birthday

When he was still a little lad,
A dream lived in his soul;
To make the world a better place,
And broken people whole.

His dream became a driving force
That guided him along,
As he matured into a man,
And faith grew deep and strong.

He gave his life in service,
To preach and serve and pray;
To teach about salvation
And help to show the way.

God then smiled and whispered,
"You should not be alone,
So you shall have a helpmate
'Til life on earth is gone".

God gave to him a maiden,
So pure in heart is she,
The peace reflected in her smile
Is there for all to see.

And so together hand in hand
They face whate'er befalls;
Their faith is anchored in the Lord,
They go where'er He calls.

On this most special day of days,
May gifts of love be found;
May blessings fall like raindrops
And joy and peace abound.

October 6, 2001

For Divya, on Her Birthday

Without a fear she stepped onto
A path that was untrod;
Following a strong conviction
She had received from God.

Into her life there came someone
To love her and to care;
And the two were joined together
To work and serve and share.

In faith she chose a country
And a family yet unknown;
But they wrapped their arms around her
And claimed her as their own.

She charmed whoever met her
With her beauty and her smile;
And she embraced their friendship
Without pretense or guile.

It's time for her to celebrate,
A year has come and gone;
And she will raise a cup of joy
With those she calls her own.

May heaven's windows open
And many blessings pour
On one who is most special,
On one whom we adore.

October 16, 2001

Nathaniel

When dawn's first light dispels the night
And heralds a brand new day,
An eager young lad arises,
All ready to work or play.
A promise does each hour hold
Of discovering something new;
With enthusiastic fervor,
That's what he'll try to do.
He is loving, kind and helpful,
And his energy has no end;
Whether playing with little sister
Or being with a special friend.
He loves to go to Grandma's house
And help her when she cooks;
Or sit and read together
From a great big pile of books.
God used a unique pattern
To create this precious treasure;
And all of those who share his life
Are blessed beyond all measure.

April, 2010

Abigail

She's a beautiful little princess
With long black, flowing hair;
And eyes so big and rich and brown
That people stop and stare.
She's quick and bright and full of life,
Each day is full of pleasure;
A book to read, a game to play,
Or finding some new treasure.
She adores her older brother;
They laugh and play and run,
Whenever they're together,
Everything they do is fun.
May life bring her great joy and love,
And all her plans succeed;
May God direct her every step
And fulfill every need.

April, 2010

High-School Poems

(1945-1947)

Rain

The rain is falling o'er the town
Like a sweet toned lullaby,
That soothes me with its gentle sound
As a word from Him on High.

The brown Earth sucks its with hungry lips,
Thirsty trees raise their leafy arms,
Buttercups drink it in dainty sips
And laugh at its refreshing charms.

Like a promise the rain did fall,
And fulfilled, it seeks to find
A place from which it heard a call,
And it goes, with its tears left behind.

The Storm

The sky is dark and restless,
Rolling clouds are drawing neigh,
The wind is blowing stronger
And the willows bend and sigh.

A tiny bird struggles against the wrath
Of the strong, forthcoming storm,
And is twisted and turned, as if shaken
By a great, invisible arm.

Suddenly for a moment, all is deathly still,
There is not a breath of sound,
Then with a crash, the storm breaks loose,
As if the wind, a target had found.

The rain comes down in torrents
That fills the rivers and sea,
And comes silently sliding down the hill
As if coming in reach of me.

Then just as suddenly as it began,
The fury of the storm goes by,
All nature comes out of hiding,
Unveiled by the sun in the sky.

My Home Town

I wouldn't exchange my little home town
For city so noisy and bright.
In my little home town there's not much sound
And the stars give us plenty of light.

The city has beautiful places
Like museums or bright city halls,
But give me the wide open spaces,
It's more beautiful than skyscrapers tall.

In the little home town that I cherish,
Where friends are faithful and true
I want to live 'til I perish,
Under skies that are always blue.

A Faithful Servant

A truly great servant of Him
Who watches o'er us from above,
He talks to his people and tells them
Of the wonders of God and His love

Without complaint, he talks and works,
Receiving strength from the Master and Friend,
Asking for no fee, not one duty he shrinks,
He'll work for his Lord to the end.

Always trying to save a lost soul
And bring him to the cross,
Always trying to add to the roll
A saved sinner,where there once was a loss.

Surely some day, he will look on God's face,
And humbly kneel at His throne,
When he is called to that Heavenly place,
And the last of life's suffering is gone.

"Inspired by a truly great servant of God, Reverend G. P. Comer,
and written by a faithful admirer of his."

Wava Lee Caddenhead

Oh, But to Have a Brain!

Oh, but to have a brain,
One that would think real good,
Then people would know I'm not so dumb,
I'd show them if I could.

I'd have all the answers ready,
At school or any place.
then I wouldn't have to stop and guess
And teachers I wouldn't disgrace.

There's just nothing I wouldn't know,
Except one thing, and I guess
That it takes more than just old brains
To make a boy friend say "Yes"!

The Moment I Love Best

The sun was slowly sinking
O'er a mountain in the west,
When I thought about the day
And the moment I loved the best.

Was it when I was with friends,
Laughing, acting Oh, so gay?
No, that was not the time
I loved best of the day.

Was it when I helped someone?
No, I still couldn't say.
That it was the happiest moment
I had spent during the day.

Suddenly, I knew no doubt
The best moment of the day,
It was the time this morning
When I humbly knelt to pray.

The Monster

Licking up the miles with a scorching tongue
It travels on and on;
Searching every living thing,
Touching all with its searing breath.

Relentlessly, with steady purpose
It beats upon the earth,
Until the flowers droop their heads
And trees murmur in protest.

For a moment it hides behind a cloud
As if to rest from its mad race,
Then, like a monster it goes rushing out,
Showing the world it is the SUN.

The Wind, My Friend

The wind is whistling 'round my door,
It wants to get inside,
I have heard it talk before,
It moaned and called and cried.

It chills me with it's icy hand,
And haunts my night and day,
Chasing itself o'er all the land,
Luring me out to play.

I pull my collar near my ears,
And bravely try to show,
That it's the least of all my fears
But the truth it seems to know.

Through the winter I'll struggle on
As I have done before,
Until this chilling wind is gone
And I am warm once more.

Lon Morris Poems

(1947-1949)

Autumn Signs

When I awoke this morning
The air was crisp and clear,
It had that certain feeling
That fall is almost here.
The summer joys have vanished
Sweet thoughts are filed away
And young eager hearts are waiting
The birth of an autumn day.
New visions are crazily whirling,
Of college so soon begun,
Popcorn, balls, that ripping thrill
When the first big game is won;
Donning a skirt and sweater
That smell of musty moth balls
Outing again the nostalgia
That an old loved song still recalls.
These evening walks in the moonlight
The gaudy sights of the fair;
The tingling, fresh, spicy odor
Of burning leaves in the air.
Hoary frost on the apples,
Hearts that are happy and light
Nature has cast upon the world
A spell of Autumn delight.

To a Priceless Orchid

Like a pure and exquisite flower
Whose scarcity makes it rare
She grows more lovely each hour
With a countenance gentle and fair.
Her roots are deep in life's virgin soil,
While her petals are raised to the sun;
There she gains strength to face the day's toll
And peace when day's battles are won.
The fragrant power of her red sweet scent
Enchants and holds whom it reaches,
Yet it is but an intangible hunt,
Of the living lesson she teaches.

For Future Use

Thanks for the lovely memories
You've given me to keep,
I've placed them very gently
In my mind – put way back deep;
The memory of the lovely night
And all the things you said,
The beauty of it made me drunk;
My hungry heart is fed
I'm sure you did not realize
How much it meant to me,
The flower on my frock sent forthcoming
The fragrance of ecstasy.
Thanks for all the whirling thought
That filled my whirling mind,
They urged me on to seek new heights,
The past I left behind.
When in the winter of my life
The days seen dark and drear,
I'll slip those memories out again,
Those thought so fresh and dear,
And I'll remember long ago
That night as soft as dew,
When the stars smiled down on us.
For I fell in love with you.

Ode to Melancholy

My heart is stirred with a sweet pang of passion,
And it skips a beat in its slow dull throb,
As it feels again the same ache of longing
And the pain that brought to my throat a sob.
It remembers days that are lost forever;
Warm, happy days that were filled with peace.
And now there lies but a sad empty burning -
Oh! That my heart could find release.
Again I wander along the green pathways
That my steps have slowly moulded and worn;
Again I smell the flower's sweet nectar
And my soul, enraptured with memory, is torn.
Once more I can feel the soft gentle kisses
Of the lover who sank so oft at my feet,
And fervently swore his love would be endless
"Til he fell in the clutch of death's burning heat.
My heat stirs yet with a sweet pain of passion,
Remembering the love it often had known,
And then it slows, in cold, dismal beating,
Oh! Those moments forever have vanished and gone!

My Towers

Standing proud in early dawn,
All wrapped in clinging mist;
Her towers gleaming softly
That the moon had gently kissed.
She always stands so nobly
In all her strength and power,
With such a welcome, friendly air
The birds alight in her bower.

Through all her changing moods I've watched
In awe and contemplation,
Changing and yet so changeless
In her endless evaluation.
I've seen her in a careless mood
When the flirting breeze caressed her,
Clinging to ivy tendrils green
As though a fit possessed her.

In a gentle mood she is a queen
With the moon reflecting its beams,
When stars are encrusted overhead
As bright as youthful dreams.
I've stared while raindrops splatter
Against her soft grey wall,
And I store the sight within my hear
As a memory to recall.

She stands, a symbol of courage and truth--
Of work and praise that is just;
Her principles formed by hands of the past
And left in the future's trust.
My heart grows sad and so heavy
At thoughts of leaving my towers,
No more to sit in silent peace
And pray as I watched by the hours.

Then a comforting whisper comes
And I know that though I part
I still will have throughout my life
The towers in my heart.

The Unholy Four

Mere words cannot express the things
I really want to say,
And so I'll just say "Thank you"
In the same old simple way.
Thank you for the lovely time
You arranged for us to share,
The food you brought was yummy
And there was lots to spare.
The gifts for Mrs. Peeples
Were well planned and so sweet;
And listening to her reminisce
Was a very special treat.

When we saw our Alma Mater,
So changed and yet so dear,
It brought back precious memories
And a sentimental tear.
We are so glad our paths did cross,
Your friendship is a treasure,
For you always serve your fellow man
With a love no one can measure.

Get together at Lon Morris

For Bonnie and Roy

Two hearts were bound together
And the wedding vows were said,
Two rings then sealed the promise
As Roy and Bonnie wed.

Together, hand in hand they faced
The future with no fears;
Vowing to face each challenge
That faced them through the years.

With breathless speed did time go by,
And life was full of joy.
Two precious girls soon came along,
And then a little boy.

Often came laughter; sometimes came tears,
 But faith was strong and sure,
And they both knew without a doubt
Their commitment would endure.

Two score and four years now have passed
Since first they said, "I do",
But Roy and Bonnie know those vows
Today hold just as true.

So with great love and joy we toast
Two friends we dearly love,
With wishes for great times ahead,
And God's blessings from above.

For Bill and Relta

On a magic day in August,
Two lives joined to be as one;
They vowed e'er to walk together
From the dawn to setting sun.

Unafraid they faced the future
Walking pathways yet untrod;
Hand in hand they walked together,
Hand in His, they walked with God.

Half a century they've experienced,
Fashioned by their joys and tears;
And still lingering, sweet and tender
Are dear memories of those years.

Although pain and disappointments
Much too often came their way,
They held fast to vows they'd taken,
Vows to serve their God each day.

Twilight years are now approaching,
Soon life's shadows will be near;
But this day they are surrounded
By all those whom they hold dear.

Son and daughter and their spouses,
Sweet grandchildren all aglow;
Friends and kin are here in masses
With warm greetings to bestow.

May God's love most richly bless them,
May His Spirit give them peace;
May their troubles melt like raindrops,
May their laughter never cease.

With much affection,
Wava Fick
August 4, 2001

For Mary Lou

She has reached another milestone
In her busy and bustling life;
A life of fruitful service
As teacher, as mother, as wife.

To know her is to love her,
She is a loyal friend;
Somehow a smile from her will help
A broken heart to mend.

She has walked a path of goodness
And scattered precious seeds
Of joy and hope and kindness
That choked out evil's weeds.

She has earned a time of quiet leisure,
A time to just sit and rock;
While others bring her some iced tea
And she puts away the old clock.

But nay, that's not in her nature,
She'll find a path yet untrod,
Or lead someone who has wandered
Back to the throne of our God.

So we can only stand in awe
And hope to match her stride,
 She may have reached three score and ten,
But she acts like she's one score nine!

Love and kisses,
Wava Fick
September 30, 2000

Memories

Thanks for the memories of
      a time that now is gone;
And so we've come to claim once more
      those days that were our own.
Do you recall when first you saw
      the towers, tall and strong?
And in your heart you truly knew,
      it's here where you belong.
Meeting teachers, making friends,
      life was a hectic pace;
Kissing Elmer, Morning Watch,
      each ritual had its place.
Walking to church on Sunday,
      and nodding in the pew;
On the menu for lunch was chicken,
      as everybody knew.
Remember going to Sadlers?
      That was the place to meet;
Root beer floats, studying our notes,
      just being there was a treat.
Yes, thanks for the memory
      of banquets and wiener roasts.
When the Bearcat team won Championships,
      we yelled and gave them toasts.
Those walks down Honeysuckle Lane
      when romance filled the air
Resulted in future weddings,
      for love first blossomed there.

And now we toast those happy days,
        when we were young and free,
When we were challenged to become
        what we were meant to be.
We are indebted to this school
        we've all come back to see;
So now we lift our glasses!
        Lon Morris, hail to thee!

Wava Lee (Caddenhead) Fick
April 24, 1999

Reflections on Life

Though our hair has turned to silver,
And our mouths are full of gold;
Don't tell us we are slowing down
Or that we're growing old.

For we are young in spirit,
We still know how to smile;
And we will only choose the things
That make our lives worthwhile.

We cherish the friends who love us
In good times and in bad;
Who celebrate our victories
And cry when we are sad.

For more than half a century
Eight friends have sealed a bond
Of love that will be lasting
In this life and beyond.

We pray that God will grant us
More years to share this love;
'Til we have that great reunion
When we meet in heaven above.

March 11, 2001
Wava Fick

Memories on the Occasion
of a Fifty-Year Reunion

In the fall of '47, four anxious, starry eyed girls
Left their homes for a good education
And to seek life's oyster of pearls.
A daring adventure, with more faith than funds,
And a step onto paths yet untrod;
They each started forth on separate paths,
Soon to walk on Lon Morris sod.

A modest church school in a quiet sleepy town,
Who could guess at the strength and the power
That was hidden so deep within its walls,
And that stretched to the top of its tower.
Kindness and love were discovered there,
And a faith that proved strong and sure;
Laughter and tears and dark, hidden fears
Were shared, knowing trust would endure.

Now, fifty years have come and gone
As swiftly as the blink of an eye;
And the friendship formed by four special friends
Grew so strong it never could die.

Dear Relta, the senior of the four
Inspired and challenged us all;
She was blessed by a roommate named Bonnie,
Whose mischief we still can recall.

Then there was Wava Lee, naive and scared,
But Mary Lou was her teacher;
She lifted Wava whenever she fell,
She knew just how to reach her.

With Lon Morris ended, the four went away
To finish that which they'd begun,
Wondering if ever again they would meet...
Or if memories would fade like the sun.

To San Marcos went Relta, and to her delight
The man of her dreams she did meet.
His first name was Bill, and he surely did fill
Her life in a way that was sweet.
The two duly wed and went on to serve
Their church with honor and love;
Keith and Karen were born, enhancing their lives,
While their Father smiled down from above.

Now their lives are still full as many things pull
In this direction or that;
Bill still is employed and church is enjoyed,
And they each wear a grandparent hat.
But they don't complain, it's a fat gravy train
Compared to those days of old;
And their lives now are filled with family and friends,
More precious than silver or gold.

To Southwestern went Bonnie, to get her degree
Then down to south Texas she went,
And while she was there, her love she did share
So she wed the man that God sent.
Roy High is his name, and Bonnie's life changed,
For he filled it with laughter and joy;
Two sweet girls they had and they were so glad,
They had Kelly, the solitaire boy.
Now their lives are enriched by grandchildren galore,
And their travels keep them on the go,
All their days are now spent in quiet content
And pleasures of life seem to grow.

With Sam Houston behind, Mary Lou's eyes did shine
As she thought of the work that she chose;
At the Wesley House Center, she was a mentor,
A teacher and healer of woes.
Then one blessed day the Lord sent her way
Charles Danheim, who melted her heart;
Full of charm, fair of face, with melodious voice
She knew they never could part.
Ere long she knew life as a minister's wife,
With all its sorrows and joys;
Then a baby girl came, Luraleen was her name,
Soon joined by three handsome boys.
Then years went too fast, but memories last
Of the blessings so richly bestowed;
Now they've slowed down near Mt Enterprise town,
With travel and grandkids their speed;
But a welcome mat's spread and there's a warm bed

If ever someone has a need.

To T.U. went Wava, and Leroy soon came,
But two years the Army did need;
At last came the day when things went their way,
And life got quite busy, indeed!
Seven children were born, five girls and two boys;
The last when the first was but ten,
Love was abundant, though money was scarce,
But they vowed they would do it again.

On this special day we are gathered again,
Four couples whose friendship is bound.
Through heartache and pain, through
           sunshine and rain,
The threads of love have been wound
May God by his grace, 'til we see His face,
Give us many more years we can share;
May contentment increase, may our
           smiles never cease
As we each put ourself in God's care.

Wava Fick
September, 1997

Birthday Musings

Age is but an illusion,
Or so that's what I've been told;
So merely to look at the numbers
Won't prove that one has grown old.

We; cherish our most special friendship
And all those times through the years
When we can be together
To share all our joys and our tears.

All totaled, our birth years would number
Five centuries and then a bit more;
And the time left to us will be busy
As we greet all that life has in store.

It's time now to honor the birthdays
Of Carl and Bonnie and Bill;
In March they aged just a little,
But they sure aren't over the hill.

Seventy and seven in April
For Relta will be a mile stone;
And she like us, will be asking,
Where have those other years gone?

September is the magic time
For Charles and Mary Lou;
They share a common birthday month
And a love that's lasting and true.

Roy made an October debut,
But he's special each day;
He lives with a chronic "condition"
That never does get in his way.

Along in November came Wava,
Just trying to look for her place;
For the record, she still keeps on searching
But now at a much slower pace.

As a fine wine will mellow with aging,
So we are now in our prime;
And if we could bottle our wisdom,
We'd all be ahead of our time!

Wava Fick
April 10, 2003

Church Friends

Play It Again, Maestro!

We have our very own Maestro,
And we are truly blessed;
There are many skilled musicians,
But we surely have the best.

Dr. Zercher is his title,
But at our church he's Randy;
Making music is his game,
From Rock to Bach he's handy.

Sweet harmony fills the choir loft
When his baton is raised,
And angels join in the chorus
When our dear Lord is praised.

We cherish these ten years with him,
Our minister and our friend;
So play it again, Sir Maestro
May your music never end!

For Sarah

Born with music in her soul
To bless each one who hears;
She makes the spirit lift in praise
And soothes away dark fears.

Her fingers move like magic
To create an awesome sound,
That speaks of lofty places
Where hope and peace abound.

Her talent is consecrated
To Him whose power reigns;
And His glory is reflected
In her worshipful refrains.

So blessed are we who listen
And claim her as our own;
The joy she brings will linger,
Though the music may be gone.

A score and five years now have passed
Since first she came our way;
May she be granted many more
To live and love and play.

December 9, 2001
For Sarah Winkle

A Tribute to Blanche

With quiet strength her life is spent
In service born of love;
Heeding the whisper of an inner voice
That comes from the Father above.

With boundless energy she works and plans,
Her commitment has no end;
She always goes the second mile
For her church or for a friend.

While leading Westbury's women,
She gives of her talent and time;
Reaching beyond all the boundaries
And looking for new hills to climb.

God whispers, "Well done faithful servant,
On you my blessings will flow,
For you have answered my calling
And are helping my Kingdom to grow."

With one accord all the women
Rise up to call her blessed
When the Lord called her to walk with us,
He chose the very best.

Wava Fick
December 5, 1995

Sometimes we pause and reminisce
Of the things we've had and the things we miss,
And we overlook, or just forget
To appreciate what we have yet.

So as I think of all I've had,
Some things good and some things bad,
A special friend comes to my mind,
One so loving, good and kind.

For those who need her, she is there
To give unselfish, tender care.
Forgetting self, she walks in love,
Receiving strength from God above.

God saw a need, so he sent Boo
To spread His love and witness, too;
Those who know her are so blessed,
For when God sent her, he gave His best!

For Boo Hatfield

Friends at the

United Methodist Center

Sweet Genny, with a smile so bright
It makes the roses grow;
Dear Genny, with a heart of love,
Where did you get that glow?
Do you have a lovely secret
That's meant for you alone?
Or did you learn a wondrous truth
That you had never known?

You are such a gentle lady,
So full of gifts and graces;
Spreading joy and brightness
In all the darkest places.
To know you is to love you,
We're glad God sent you here
To be the special angel
That tells us He is near.

Wava Fick
August, 1999

Arlene, you've said you want to leave
This world of work behind;
And set your hands to other tasks
That you may have in mind.
Nearly six years you've been here,
And how the time did fly;
But now you have decided
That you must say goodbye.
We know you love to work at church,
And knit and sew and cook;
Or spend a rainy afternoon
Just buried in a book.
But playing Grandma is the job
That rates above the rest;
Trips and bridge and Garden Club
Just come in second best.
But think of all the things you'll miss
When you are here no more;
Those lovely trips to Lakeview;
Bulk mailings by the score.
Those endless Boards and Agencies
That always stay to eat;
Switchboard duty, Conference fun. . .
They made your job complete!

Arlene, we hate to see you go,
And you have heard us muse;
But if we could, we surely would
Be right there in your shoes!

GOOD LUCK!

Wava
July 29, 1983

Arlene Little
Methodist Center

There once was a preacher named Bill
Who thought he was over the hill,
So he said, "I'll retire and pursue my desire
To travel, take pictures and such.

Now Janet is Bill's loving wife,
And surely the light of his life,
But she asked, "Can I cope - and is there any hope
When he thinks he's over the hill".

Bill still whacks a tennis ball high,
And he's still got a gleam in his eye,
But between you and me, and I think you'll agree,
That gleam doesn't beam quite so bright.

Yes, Bill is still young at heart,
But his battery takes longer to start,
Now the mileage is showing,
          but the motor's still going
And he hasn't yet run out of gas.

You may say if you dare that Bill's old,
That the lines on his face are quite bold;
 But don't ever say Bill is over the hill,
He's still trying to climb to the top!

Bill Scales on Retirement

You are leaving us here for the Isle of fun
Where there's lots of sea and surf and sun;
Where the tourists come and their money goes,
And all day long the sea wind blows.
You can take a stroll along the Strand
Or wriggle your toes in the warm Gulf sand;
You can lie on the beach all slathered with lotion
And read a good book, if you take the notion.
You might even write one, if it strikes your fancy,
There's lots to do if you start getting antsy.
But Moody is foremost in your mind,
And there is where you'll, surely find
The joy of serving your fellow man
And ministering in every way you can.
But best of all you can preach the Word
And know God's message will be heard
In a church majestic in its beauty,
Where tradition was built on a sense of duty.
When you come into your kingdom
         and are living in paradise,
Remember us you left behind,
         at least just once or twice!
Just say the word and we'll be all be there
         to make the fun begin,
We'll have a great beach party
         And then we'll go hang ten!

Bob Parrot as he left the Methodist S.W. District for Moody
Memorial in Galveston

96

Some folks might think it's tough at the top,
With telephones ringing and projects that flop;
Where questions are asked and answers aren't found,
And everyone rides on a merry-go-round.
This may be true but there is a way
To ride with the punches and hang loose each day;
A certain D. S. has learned how to cope,
Instead of defeat, he always finds hope.
A keen sense of humor quite often he shows,
Where he finds his jokes, no one ever knows;
He just loves to tease and make someone smile,
And he's always willing to go one more mile.
Beyond reproach, his integrity stands,
He listens to what his conscience demands;
And yet his sense of justice is strong,
He won't hesitate to fight something wrong.
We're glad Carroll came to guide the Southwest,
When leadership counts, he's one of the best;
And though it's his birthday,
        which one we don't know;
'Cause he's young at heart and his age doesn't show!
HAPPY BIRTHDAY!

Carroll Fancher, Methodist Center

A Tribute to Our Bosses

While phones are ringing off the walls
And preachers sitting in the halls
Waiting for their chance to air
Some little problem - if they dare!
Behind closed doors our boss may sit,
Hearing someone throw a fit!
With Solomon's wisdom and the patience of Job,
He may put on a Judge's robe
And solve a problem, or dry a tear,
Or help to pray away some fear.
The Good Book guides our bosses' lives,
They preach good sermons and love their wives;
They treat us kind and rarely fuss,
And never do you hear one cuss!
So we can understand and smile
When asked to go the second mile;
And we will do our best to please
When we hear statements such as these:
"Pick up someone who's in town;
Take a group of kids around;
Buy some stamps, serve a lunch,
Also coffee and some punch.
Make 500 copies, now!
Get bulk mailing done somehow.
Where's the film I need tonight?
These figures do not balance right!
That pension form just can't be found;
Room to Grow must find new ground."

We know we are appreciated,
You make us feel quite highly rated;
But if you want to please us most,
You don't have to brag or boast,
You don't have to sing our praises,
You can just give us all raises!

www.ingramcontent.com/pod-product-compliance
Lightning Source LLC
Chambersburg PA
CBHW020949030426
42339CB00004B/25